The Scopes Monkey Trial: The History of 20th Century America's Most Famous Court Case

By Charles River Editors

A picture of court proceedings going on outside the courthouse

About Charles River Editors

Charles River Editors provides superior editing and original writing services in the digital publishing industry, with the expertise to create digital content for publishers across a vast range of subject matter. In addition to providing original digital content for third party publishers, we also republish civilization's greatest literary works, bringing them to new generations of readers via ebooks.

Sign up here to receive updates about free books as we publish them, and visit Our Kindle Author Page to browse today's free promotions and our most recently published Kindle titles.

Introduction

The Scopes Trial

"I never had any idea my bill would make a fuss. I just thought it would become a law, and that everybody would abide by it and that we wouldn't hear any more of evolution in Tennessee." – John Washington Butler

In the early 20th century, Darwin's theory of evolution was still a relative novelty, but it had spurred some Americans to react by preventing it from being taught in schools, including in Tennessee, which passed the Butler Act to prohibit teaching the theory in a state-funded school. This set the stage for proponents of the theory to challenge the law by having a teacher bring up Darwin's theory in a classroom, which is how a little known substitute teacher named John Scopes had his name attached to one of the most famous cases in American history.

Although it is best known as the Scopes Trial or Scopes Monkey Trial even 90 years later, the case was intentionally created as a test case, and from the beginning it was meant to draw attention not just to the issue but to the small town of Dayton, Tennessee itself. In that, it succeeded, not simply because the case was important but because it brought William Jennings Bryan, one of America's most famous politicians, to participate. Bryan would square off against renowned lawyer Clarence Darrow, who would represent Scopes in the proceedings.

While the case was technically challenging a law and proceeded like a normal trial, including an appeal to Tennessee's Supreme Court, the Scopes Monkey Trial was essentially a national debate on theology, science, and each one's place in the classroom. The trial is best known not necessarily for the results but for the rhetorical arguments that were made on each side, and for the manner in which Darrow and Bryan squared off. In perhaps the most famous scene of the entire affair, Darrow actually cross-examined Bryan himself.

Naturally, the case was politically charged on all sides, and even the judge was conspicuously biased against Scopes' defense, but Scopes successfully appealed the fine at the Tennessee Supreme Court. Still, the issue remained heated even after, especially when Bryan died shortly after the trial.

The Scopes Monkey Trial: The History of 20th Century America's Most Famous Court Case analyzes the background and proceedings of the case. Along with pictures of important people, places, and events, you will learn about the Scopes Monkey Trial like never before.

The Scopes Monkey Trial: The History of 20th Century America's Most Famous Court Case

About Charles River Editors

Introduction

Chapter 1: The Forthcoming Trial

"Such obscenities as the forthcoming trial of the Tennessee evolutionist, if they serve no other purpose, at least call attention dramatically to the fact that enlightenment, among mankind, is very narrowly dispersed. It is common to assume that human progress affects everyone -- that even the dullest man, in these bright days, knows more than any man of, say, the Eighteenth Century, and is far more civilized. This assumption is quite erroneous. The men of the educated minority, no doubt, know more than their predecessors, and of some of them, perhaps, it may be said that they are more civilized -- though I should not like to be put to giving names -- but the great masses of men, even in this inspired republic, are precisely where the mob was at the dawn of history. They are ignorant, they are dishonest, they are cowardly, they are ignoble. They know little if anything that is worth knowing, and there is not the slightest sign of a natural desire among them to increase their knowledge. Such immortal vermin, true enough, get their share of the fruits of human progress, and so they may be said, in a way, to have their part in it." - H. L. Mencken

The Scopes Monkey Trial took place about as early as it could've been, because only a few months earlier in 1925, there would not have been any problem with what John Thomas Scopes taught. Ironically, *Hunter's Civic Biology*, Rhea County High School's official science textbook, was the most widely used text in the United States and clearly taught a Darwinian view of the origin of man. In fact, all the textbooks used in United States schools at that time were Darwinian in their perspective. However, just a few months earlier, on March 23, the Governor of Tennessee signed into law a bill known as the Butler Act: "An act prohibiting the teaching of the Evolution Theory in all the Universities, Normals and all other public schools of Tennessee, which are supported in whole or in part by the public school funds of the State, and to provide penalties for the violations thereof…That it shall be unlawful for any teacher in any of the Universities, Normals and all other public schools of the State which are supported in whole or in part by the public school funds of the State, to teach any theory that denies the story of the Divine Creation of man as taught in the Bible, and to teach instead that man has descended from a lower order of animals."

At the time, most people saw the act as a symbolic law that would never be enforced. As historian Lawrence Levine observed, "the anti-evolution law didn't change anything. It didn't change anything, and yet it was important to pass it, not because it was going to -- they had textbooks in Tennessee, which taught evolution. So any teacher who used those textbooks had to teach evolution. The importance of that -- it was a symbolic law. It was a law symbolizing who was right, who was legitimate. Religion was legitimate. Darwin was not legitimate in the state of Tennessee."

In fact, the law might never have been enforced, and a person may never have been prosecuted for violating it, had it not been for the newly formed American Civil Liberties Union (ACLU).

The ACLU placed advertisements in a number of Tennessee newspapers encouraging teachers to challenge the law and assuring them of the ACLU's support of their cases. George Rappleyea, a New York lawyer hired to manage the bankruptcy of the failing businesses in little Dayton, saw one of the advertisements and had an idea which he shared with a friend that he had ironically met at church. John Thomas Scopes was a 24-year-old teacher at Rhea County High School who had only recently moved to Dayton from his hometown in Illinois, and he wasn't even hired primarily to teach science but to coach football. However, Rappleyea knew of Scopes' interest in Darwin's work, and both the men knew that even their own pastor believed in Darwin's theories, leading them to believe that there was no real conflict between their faith and science.

Scopes

Rappleyea

Rappleyea and Scopes

Thus, Rappleyea aimed to persuade Scopes to challenge the Butler Act, and that they could work together to have the test case tried in Dayton and bring the town a much needed shot of publicity and financial infusion. He quickly arranged a meeting with F.E. Robinson, the owner of a struggling drugstore next door to the Aqua Hotel. According to historian Edward J. Larson, "Robinson at the time was chairman of the local school board and his downtown drug store had a soda fountain that served as the watering hole for the business and professional elite of town back then. … [Rappleyea] ran down there and told them his scheme." Rappleyea convinced Robinson that if the school board would just arrest one of its teachers for teaching what was already in the textbook, that teacher's trial would bring people pouring into town and spark a tourism industry that would be a huge boon.

Robinson

Robinson agreed with the plan, and the two men contacted Scopes and invited him to become the accused. By the time he got to the drugstore, most of the town leaders were already there, waiting to talk to him. Ironically, Scopes could not even remember if he had actually taught the theory of evolution in class, but it seemed likely to him that he had since he had gone through the textbook. Thus, he agreed, telling the men, "If you can prove that I've taught evolution and that I can qualify as a defendant, then I'll be willing to stand trial." Rappleyea called the local Sheriff and swore out a warrant against Scopes, who by that time had left and returned to the tennis court where he had been before being interrupted to take his place in history.

With that, School Superintendent Walter White wasted no time in contacting the *Chattanooga*

Times and telling a reporter, "Something has happened that's going to put Dayton on the map!" Eloise Reed, a teenager in Dayton at the time, later recalled, "The town was buzzing with excitement. Not over the trial but over all of the people coming to town."

As things were put in motion, Scopes got in touch with some of his students and explained what was going on, encouraging them to testify against him. Based on the testimony of three teens that he had indeed taught evolutionary principles in class, Scopes was indicted by the grand jury on May: "The grand jurors for the state aforesaid, being duly summoned, elected, empaneled, sworn, and charged to inquire for the body of the county aforesaid, upon their oaths present: That John Thomas Scopes, heretofore on the 24th day of April, 1925, in the county aforesaid, then and there, unlawfully did willfully teach in the public schools of Rhea county, Tennessee, which said public schools are supported in part and in whole by the public school fund of the- state, a certain theory and theories that deny the story of the divine creation of man as taught in the Bible, and did teach instead thereof that man has descended from a lower order of animals, he, the said John Thomas Scopes, being at the time, or prior thereto, a teacher in the public schools of Rhea county, Tennessee, aforesaid, against the peace and dignity of the state." Paul Patterson, who then owned the *Baltimore Sun*, put up the $500 the court set for Scopes' bail.

The trial was set for July, and newsmen from around the country and the rest of the world began making plans to be in Dayton for the big event. Hollywood sent photographers with newsreel cameras, and a telegraph company rented a local grocery store for its Main Street operations center. WGN Radio even announced that it would be broadcasting live from the trial, the first time in history that such a thing had happened. H. L. Mencken, the popular editor of the *American Mercury* magazine and a writer for the *Baltimore Sun*, was said to have arrived in town with a typewriter and four bottles of scotch. So many were coming into Dayton that the Aqua Hotel, only months earlier desperate for visitors, was having to turn people away.

Chapter 2: Human Progress

"Every step in human progress, from the first feeble stirrings in the abyss of time, has been opposed by the great majority of men. Every valuable thing that has been added to the store of man's possessions has been derided by them when it was new, and destroyed by them when they had the power. They have fought every new truth ever heard of, and they have killed every truth-seeker who got into their hands. … We must think of human progress, not as of something going on in the race in general, but as of something going on in a small minority, perpetually beleaguered in a few walled towns. Now and then the horde of barbarians outside breaks through, and we have an armed effort to halt the process. That is, we have a Reformation, a French Revolution, a war for democracy, a Great Awakening. The minority is decimated and driven to cover. But a few survive -- and a few are enough to carry on." - H. L. Mencken

The Scopes trial, as *The State of Tennessee v. John Thomas Scopes* came to be known as, was in many ways the product of a time and place unique to that moment in American history. For one thing, it was the first trial to be covered by widespread media, including radio broadcasts and newsreel footage, which meant the entire country would be able to follow the trial and everyone could weigh in on what they thought the outcome should be. Also, there was much more on trial than just what would be taught; in the minds of many, the whole Progressive movement of the 1920s, complete with its flappers and speakeasies, was being held up to question. Naturally, both those for and against the loosening of traditional moral customs and norms desperately wanted to win.

There were hundreds of people in and around the Rhea County Courthouse by the time the trial began, including teachers, bootleggers, preachers and parents. There were also some unusual characters one would not expect to see at a trial in a small Southern town. As historian Edward Larson pointed out, "The Dayton civic leaders could hardly believe their good fortune. They had anticipated a great trial. They wanted a media event from the beginning. But they had never even dreamed in their wildest dreams about having the like of William Jennings Bryan and Clarence Darrow, two of the most famous orators in American history, coming together." When the American public learned that these two judicial giants would be going toe to toe in the little town of Dayton, interest turned into frenzy and the city fathers became the city's saviors.

Then there was the judge, John T. Raulston, from Jasper, Tennessee, a man with a typical all-American sort of Christian faith who strode into the courtroom each morning carrying a large, worn Bible under his arm. He would be up for reelection the following year and wanted very much to retain his position as the circuit judge for Southeastern Tennessee. He knew that this trial, and the attention is would bring, could only help his career, and some believed that he saw himself as chosen by God for this particular moment in history.

Raulston

The Rhea County Courthouse

People weren't the only ones in attendance. The crowds often included Joe Mendi, a chimpanzee who, according to Eloise Reed, "would have a little hat on…a suit on with a vest." She added, "Joe Mendi was a little fellow and his keeper was a lady. And she would bring him up to the courthouse every day and would dress him in a different suit. And of course we were always excited about seeing Joe."

Joe Mendi

All of the attention immediately began to wear on Scopes, who later admitted, "The town was filled with men and women who considered the case a duel to the death. Everything I did was likely to be noted." Scopes no doubt found that ironic, because as far as he was concerned, he was little more than a pawn in the hands of other men with varying agendas. Indeed, while he was the defendant who had his name in the case, no one in the courtroom was as well-known as the two attorneys called upon to prosecute and defend him: William Jennings Bryan and Clarence Darrow. As one historian pointed out, "You take the American personality, if there is such a thing, and divide it in two and you get Clarence Darrow and William Jennings Bryan."

A picture of Darrow and Bryan talking during the trial

Bryan had already run for president three times and served as Secretary of State under Woodrow Wilson by the time he arrived in Dayton to prosecute Scopes. He once famously claimed, "All the ills from which America suffers, can be traced to the teaching of evolution." He was a devout Christian and believe that the Bible was indeed the inerrant Word of God. He also believed that the teachings of Christ, properly applied, could have the same positive effects on America that they had had on Rome 2,000 years earlier. Historian Lawrence Levine explained, "He always mixed religion and politics. He couldn't conceive of one without the other because religion to him was the basis of politics. Without religion there could be no desire to change in a positive way. Why should anyone want to do that? Why should anyone want to be good and do good to his or her fellow human beings if -- if there was no reward afterwards, if there was no religious -- if we were just brutes? If we were just animals...why should anyone be good?

Clarence Darrow was considered the best criminal defense attorney in the country and had volunteered to defend Scopes, and the cause, as soon as he learned of the trial. He had grown up in Kinsman, Ohio, and he was known as a rapid reader and the town atheist. He was also the progressive's progressive, once opining that society "is nothing less than organized injustice."

For Darrow, the biggest appeal of the case was the opportunity to face off against Bryan. Both men were fantastic orators and in many ways the last of a breed, with Bryan rumored to have a voice that could be heard a full quarter mile away. They had also once been close friends but had parted ways over, of all things, matters of faith and religion. While Darrow embraced the 1920s, a time, according to F. Scott Fitzgerald, "when the parties were bigger, the pace was faster, and the morals were looser," Bryan was horrified by it.

A picture of Darrow during the trial

Though their names were the famous ones, each man was backed up by a team of attorneys. Joining Bryan in prosecuting the case was his own son, William Jennings Bryan, Jr., a Georgetown graduate; Ben G. McKenzie and his son, Gordon; brothers Herbert and Sue Hicks; and Tom Stewart, Tennessee's state attorney general for Rhea County. Joining Darrow on the defense team were Arthur Garfield Hays from the ACLU; Dudley Malone, a divorce lawyer; and John Neal, an eccentric lawyer and the defense's official counsel.

Hays

Neal and Scopes

The Scopes trial began in a blistering hot courtroom in Dayton, Tennessee on July 10, 1925. As Scopes himself remembered, "Dayton in 1925 was as hot as any hell the white-headed evangelist, T.T. Martin, might have conjured up. It was midsummer; the sun baked the sidewalks and its heat boiled into the courtroom, becoming a constant source of annoyance and discomfort. By the time court convened each morning around nine o'clock, the sun was already high, and by noon the room on the second floor was so ovenlike that collars wilted right along with their wearers."

When the trial finally began at 9:00 a.m. that morning, the entire town of Dayton had become one big circus, and the courthouse was the center ring. One reporter on the scene wrote, "The crowd filled the aisles, the windows, the doors. Photographers and movie men perched on chairs, tables and ladders and more than a hundred newspaper and magazine writers were cramped at a pine table set with muffled telegraph instruments and typewriters, while a radio announcer pushed through the crush of counsel to set his microphone for the edification and amusement of his radio patrons!"

John Williams of WGN in Chicago recalled, "WGN Radio received the rights to rearrange the way the courtroom was set up. And this was the first time this has happened where the media manipulates an event literally the way it's played out. Where will the people sit, where will the jury be seated? The relationship of the judge to the prosecution and the defense, all of that changed to accommodate the radio station's microphones." Several decades before television, Quinn Ryan, WGN's announcer, offered color commentary on every moment of the trial, beginning with the following remarks: "Here comes William Jennings Bryan. He enters now. His bald pate like a sunrise over Key West." Bryan, who had a good sense of humor, simply turned to Ryan and laughed. Then he strode over to Darrow so the two men could pose together for the cameras.

For his part, Judge Raulston set a dramatic tone for the trial by inviting a four-year-old boy up to the stand to draw the names of potential jurors out of a hat. One of Darrow's strengths lay in his ability to choose jury members who he knew would be sympathetic to his client; he considered jury selection to be a critical part of the trial process and took his time in questioning the potential jurors. Nonetheless, by the time the process was finished, the 12 jurors included "six Baptists, four Methodists, one disciple of Christ, and a single non-churchgoer." A few of them admitted that they could have no preconceived opinions about evolution because they did not know what it was.

Outside the courthouse, an intense festive feeling filled the air as entertainers sang songs about monkeys, locals sold monkey souvenirs, and people lined up to see a gorilla kept in a cage on a freight car. Describing the scene, one reporter joked, "People crowded in to contemplate whether this monster could be their kinsman. The poor brute cowered in a corner with his hands over his eyes, afraid it might be true."

After the trial ended for the day on Friday the 10th, the lawyers retired for a weekend of research and preparation for the coming week. Bryan, however, had an additional speaking engagement: an address to the congregation of the local First Methodist Church. Eloise Reed later recalled, "There wasn't even standing room in the church and people were on the outside listening to him. The windows were all open. It was a hot summer day and people had come in from everywhere. I don't know how so many people knew that he was going to be speaking... But I had a front seat that day, right in front of the pulpit where he was standing and I was sitting there in awe of him, you know... I guess I was trying to see his silver tongue that I had heard so much about."

Chapter 3: The Brunt of the First Attack

"Darrow's peroration yesterday was interrupted by Judge Raulston, but the force of it got into the air nevertheless. This year it is a misdemeanor for a country school teacher to flout the archaic nonsense of Genesis. Next year it will be a felony. The year after the net will be spread wider. Pedagogues, after all, are small game; there are larger birds to snare -- larger and juicier. ... Tennessee is bearing the brunt of the first attack simply because the civilized minority, down here, is extraordinarily pusillanimous. I have met no educated man who is not ashamed of the ridicule that has fallen upon the State, and I have met none, save only judge Neal, who had the courage to speak out while it was yet time. No Tennessee counsel of any importance came into the case until yesterday and then they came in stepping very softly as if taking a brief for sense were a dangerous matter. ... The State is smiling and beautiful, and of late it has begun to be rich. I know of no American city that is set in more lovely scenery than Chattanooga, or that has more charming homes. The civilized minority is as large here, I believe, as anywhere else. It has made a city of splendid material comforts and kept it in order." - H. L. Mencken

When court resumed on Monday, the defense came out swinging, with Darrow's co-counsel, John Neal, asking Raulston to rule the Butler Act itself unconstitutional. After Neal laid the groundwork, Darrow took over and made his first major speech of the trial, saying in part, "This case we have to argue is a case at law, and hard as it is for me to bring my mind to conceive it, almost impossible as it is to put my mind back into the sixteenth century, I am going to argue it as if it was serious, and as if it was a death struggle between two civilizations. ... We have been informed that the legislature has the right to prescribe the course of study in the public schools. Within reason, they no doubt have, no doubt. ...under the rest of the constitution if it shall remain in force in the state, could they prescribe it if the course of study was only to teach religion, because several hundred years ago, when our people believed in freedom, and when no men felt so sure of their own sophistry that they were willing to send a man to jail who did not believe them. The people of Tennessee adopted a constitution, and they made it broad and plain, and said that the people of Tennessee should always enjoy religious freedom in its broadest terms."

Darrow referred the court to an earlier Tennessee law that had been overturned and that had once said that it was a "misdemeanor for any one, engaged in the business of a barber, to shave, shampoo, cut hair, or keep open their bath-rooms on Sunday." Running with this theme, he continued, "Well, of course, I suppose it would be wicked to take a bath on Sunday, I don't know, but that was not the trouble with this statute. It would have been all right to forbid the good people of Tennessee from taking a bath on Sunday, but that was not the trouble. A barber could not give a bath on Sunday, anybody else could. No barber shall be permitted to give a bath on Sunday, and the Supreme Court seemed to take judicial notice of the fact that people take a bath on Sunday just the same as any other day. Foreigners come in there in the habit of bathing on Sundays just as any other time, and they could keep shops open, but a barber shop, no. The

Supreme Court said that would not do, you could not let a hotel get away with what a barber shop can't."

In concluding his remarks, Darrow stated, "To strangle puppies is good when they grow up into mad dogs, maybe. I will tell you what is going to happen, and I do not pretend to be a prophet, but I do not need to be a prophet to know. Your honor knows the fires that have been lighted in America to kindle religious' bigotry and hate. … If today you can take a thing like evolution and make it a crime to teach it in the public school, tomorrow you can make it a crime to teach it in the private schools, and the next year you can make it a crime to teach it to the hustings or in the church. At the next session you may ban books and the newspapers. Soon you may set Catholic against Protestant and Protestant against Protestant, and try to foist your own religion up on the minds of men. If you can do one you can do the other. Ignorance and fanaticism is ever busy and needs feeding. Always it is feeding and gloating for more. Today it is the public school teachers, tomorrow the private. The next day the preachers and the lecturers, the magazines, the books, the newspapers. After while, your honor, it is the setting of man against man and creed against creed until with flying banners and beating drums we are marching backward to the glorious ages of the sixteenth century when bigots lighted fagots to burn the men who dared to bring any intelligence and enlightenment and culture to the human mind."

Darrow later discussed the strategy behind these aggressive remarks: "I made a complete and aggressive opening in the case. I did this for the reason that we never at any stage intended to make any arguments in the case. We knew that Mr. Bryan was there to make a closing speech about 'The Prince of Peace.'"

The next day, Darrow became even more aggressive. After sitting quietly during the opening prayer offered at the beginning of each of the previous day's proceedings, he made an objection on the third day, telling the judge that "the nature of this case being one where it is claimed by the state that there is a conflict between science and religion, above all other cases there should be no part taken outside the evidence in this case and no attempt by means of prayer or in any other way to influence the deliberation and consideration of the jury of the facts in this case." Speaking on behalf of the prosecution, Tennessee Attorney General Stewart supported the prayers, asserting that "the state makes no contention, that this is a conflict between science and religion…it is quite proper to open the court with prayer if the court sees fit to do it, and such an idea extended by the agnostic counsel for the defense is foreign to the thoughts and ideas of the people who do not know anything about infidelity and care less." In the end, the court allowed the prayer, but Judge Raulston later agreed to allow the local pastor's association to choose who would offer it each day. That same day, Raulston also ruled that the law in question was constitutional and that the trial should continue.

Stewart

It was not until the afternoon of the fourth day of the trial that the court case really got moving. Scopes entered a plea of "not guilty," and Malone, speaking on behalf of the defense, told the court, "The defense contends that to convict Scopes the prosecution must prove that Scopes not only taught the theory of evolution, but that he also, and at the same time, denied the theory of creation as set forth in the Bible. The defense contends the prosecution must prove that the defendant Scopes, did these two things and that what he taught was a violation of the statute. We will prove that whether this statute be constitutional or unconstitutional the Defendant Scopes did not and could not violate it. We maintain that since the Defendant Scopes has been indicted under a statute which prohibits the teaching of the evolutionary theory, the prosecution must prove as part of the case what evolution is. … While the defense thinks there is a conflict between evolution and the Old Testament, we believe there is no conflict between evolution and Christianity. There may be a conflict between evolution and the peculiar ideas of Christianity, which are held by Mr. Bryan as the evangelical leader of the prosecution, but we deny that the evangelical leader of the prosecution is an authorized spokesman for the Christians of the United States."

Malone also accused the state of misrepresenting what evolution taught: "The prosecution has twice since the beginning of the trial referred to man as descended from monkeys. This may be the understanding of the theory of evolution of the prosecution. It is not the view, opinion or knowledge of evolution held by the defense. No scientist of any preeminent standing today holds such a view. The most that science says today is that there is an order of men like mammals which are more capable of walking erect than other animals, and more capable than other animals in the use of the forefeet as hands."

Chapter 4: Eloquent Presentations

"The high point of yesterday's proceedings was reached with the appearance of Dr. Maynard M. Metcalfe, of the Johns Hopkins. The doctor is a somewhat chubby man of bland mien, and during the first part of his testimony, with the jury present, the prosecution apparently viewed him with great equanimity. But the instant he was asked a question bearing directly upon the case at bar there was a flurry in the Bryan pen and Stewart was on his feet with protests. ... The judge then excluded the jury.... Then began one of the clearest, most succinct and withal most eloquent presentations of the case for the evolutionists that I have ever heard. The doctor was never at a loss for a word, and his ideas flowed freely and smoothly. Darrow steered him magnificently. A word or two and he was howling down the wind. Another and he hauled up to discharge a broadside. There was no cocksureness in him. Instead he was rather cautious and deprecatory and sometimes he halted and confessed his ignorance. But what he got over before he finished was a superb counterblast to the fundamentalist buncombe." - H. L. Mencken

Following these opening statements, the state then called its first witness, Walter White, ironically one of the men behind the scheme to test the case. The state attorney questioned White about his conversations concerning covering the material in the textbook and then introduced the Bible itself into evidence. This led the defense to demand that the state clarify which version of the Bible, and that the court certify it as evidence. Hays declared, "If the court should take judicial notice of this exhibit as the Bible, you must likewise take judicial notice that there are various Bibles. And the King James' version is not necessarily the Bible and when they introduce one book in evidence, we are saying there are several different books called the Bible. It is not relevant unless those books are the same. You know there is a Hebrew Bible, of some thirty nine books; and there is a Protestant Bible, and a Catholic Bible—the Protestant of sixty-six and the Catholic of eighty books; and you have the King James' version, and a revised version and there are 30,000 differences between the King James' version and it. . . .Who is to say that the King James Version is the Bible? The prosecution will have to prove what Bible it is, and they will have to state the theory as taught in the Bible, and I presume the prosecution will be able to point out which theory of the creation as taught in the Bible they relied upon in prosecuting Mr. Scopes." The court did indeed certify the King James Bible offered into evidence, since it was considered the version commonly used.

White

The state next called Howard Morgan, one of Scopes' students, who admitted, "He said that the earth was once a hot molten mass, too hot for plant or animal life to exist upon it; in the sea the earth cooled off; there was a little germ of one cell organism formed, and this organism kept evolving until it got to be a pretty good-sized animal, and then came on to be a land animal and it kept on evolving, and from this was man." The prosecution called only a few more witnesses, and after they gave similar testimony, the state rested.

When Darrow rose to call his first witness, he informed the court that he would not be calling Scopes himself to the stand because "every single word that was said against this defendant was true." Scopes later wrote, "I sat speechless, a ringside observer at my own trial, until the end of the circus…Darrow had been afraid for me to go on the stand. Darrow realized that I was not a science teacher and he was afraid that if I were put on the stand I would be asked if I actually taught biology. He knew there was a chance it could provide a traumatic setback for the defense; although I knew something of science in general, it would be quite another matter to deal exhaustively with scientific questions on the witness stand. He also knew there was nothing I could say that would benefit our cause. ... I did little more than sit, proxylike, in freedom's chair that hot, unforgettable summer—no great feat, despite the notoriety it has brought me. My role was a passive one that developed out of my willingness to test what I considered a bad law."

In fact, everyone in the courtroom must have known on some level that it was not the young teacher on trial but the relationship between religion and science. Indeed, this is what made the Scopes Trial so fascinating then and now, as it brought before a jury the very essence of what was happening in America and much of the world at that time.

Instead of Scopes, Darrow called a scientist named Maynard Metcalf as a witness. Darrow chose Metcalf carefully because the scientist was also well-known for being a Christian, and Darrow's goal was to convince the jury that the two roles were not mutually exclusive. After a few preliminary exchanges, Darrow asked, "Are you an evolutionist?" To that, Metcalf replied, "Surely, under certain circumstances that question would be an insult, under these circumstances I do not regard it as such. ... I am acquainted with practically all of the zoologists, botanists and geologists of this country who have done any work; that is, any material contribution to knowledge in those fields, and I am absolutely convinced from personal knowledge that any one of these men feel and believe, as a matter of course, that evolution is a fact, but I doubt very much if any two of them agree as to the exact method by which evolution has been brought about, but I think there is — I know there is not a single one among them who has the least doubt of the fact of evolution."

Metcalf

Darrow spent the rest of the afternoon questioning Metcalf about the details and teachings of the theory of evolution, but the jury never heard any of the testimony; since the court could not decide whether or not it was relevant to the case, the jurors had been dismissed. Of course, for their part, the jurors likely did not regret leaving the stifling courtroom and missing the exhaustive scientific lecture.

Chapter 5: Overwhelmingly Eloquent

"Malone was put up to follow and dispose of Bryan, and he achieved the business magnificently. I doubt that any louder speech has ever been heard in a court of law since the days of Gog and Magog. It roared out of the open windows like the sound of artillery practice, and alarmed the moonshiners and catamounts on distant peaks. Trains thundering by on the nearby railroad sounded faint and far away and when, toward the end, a table covered with standing and gaping journalists gave way with a crash, the noise seemed, by contrast, to be no more than a pizzicato chord upon a viola da gamba. … In brief, Malone was in good voice. It was a great day for Ireland. And for the defense. For Malone not only out-yelled Bryan, he also plainly out-generaled and out-argued him. It was simple in structure, it was clear in reasoning, and at its high points it was overwhelmingly eloquent. It was not long, but it covered the whole ground and it let off many a gaudy skyrocket, and so it conquered even the fundamentalists. At its end they gave it a tremendous cheer -- a cheer at least four times as hearty as that given to Bryan." - H. L. Mencken

The next day, the jury returned to the courtroom only to witness another lengthy argument as to whether or not they should hear the scientific testimony Darrow was preparing to continue presenting. Darrow claimed that the Butler Act only prohibited teaching that which was contrary to the teachings of the Bible and that Metcalf could demonstrate that the theory of evolution did not conflict with Biblical teaching since there were so many interpretations of it. The state countered that the Butler Act prohibited any teaching of evolutionary theory and that the only real question was whether or not Scopes had done that. Darrow countered the state's objection by saying, "We expect to show by men of science and learning—both scientists and real scholars of the Bible—men who know what they are talking about—who have made some investigation—expect to show first what evolution is, and, secondly, that any interpretation of the Bible that intelligent men could possibly make is not in conflict with any story of creation, while the Bible, in many ways, is in conflict with every known science, and there isn't a human being on earth believes it literally. We expect to show that it isn't in conflict with the theory of evolution. We expect to show what evolution is, and the interpretation of the Bible that prevails with men of intelligence who have studied it."

It was at this point that Bryan entered the fray: "The principal attorney has often suggested that I am the arch-conspirator and that I am responsible for the presence of this case and I have almost been credited with leadership of the ignorance and bigotry which he thinks could alone inspire a law like this." Bryan then went on to make the point that it was too late, at least for Scopes, to decide whether the law should exist. He continued, "[Y]ou see in this state they cannot teach the Bible. They can only teach things that declare it to be a lie, according to the learned counsel. These people in the state— Christian people—have tied their hands by their constitution. They say we believe in the Bible for it is the overwhelming belief in the state, but we will not teach that Bible, which we believe even to our children through teachers that we pay with our money. No, no, it isn't the teaching of the Bible, and we are not asking it. The question is can a minority in this state come in and compel a teacher to teach that the Bible is not true and make the parents of these children pay the expenses of the teacher to tell their children what these people believe is false and dangerous? Has it come to a time when the minority call take charge of a state like Tennessee and compel the majority to pay their teachers while they take religion out of the heart of the children of the parents who pay the teachers?"

Bryan reserved his most scathing remarks for the way in which he perceived how evolution chipped away at man's status as a superior being, "a little lower than the angels" according to the Bible: "[T]he Christian believes man came from above, but the evolutionist believes he must have come from below. And that is from a lower order of animals." Showing Judge Raulston *Hunter's* biology text, he exclaimed, "There is that book! There is the book they were teaching your children that man was a mammal and so indistinguishable among the mammals that they leave him there with thirty-four hundred and ninety-nine other mammals. Including elephants? Talk about putting Daniel in the lion's den? How dared those scientists put man in a little ring like that with lions and tigers and everything that is bad! Not only that evolution is possible, but the scientists possibly think of shutting man up in a little circle like that with all these animals, that have an odor, that extends beyond the circumference of this circle, my friends. ... Tell me that the parents of this day have not any right to declare that children are not to be taught this doctrine? Shall not be taken down from the high plane upon which God put man? Shall be detached from the throne of God and be compelled to link their ancestors with the jungle, tell that to these children? Why, my friend, if they believe it, they go back to scoff at the religion of their parents. And the parents have the right to say that no teacher paid by their money shall rob their children of faith in God and send them back to their homes, skeptical, infidels, or agnostics, or atheists."

Bryan then moved on to the case of "Leopold and Leob." A year earlier, Nathan Freudenthal Leopold, Jr. and Richard Albert Loeb, two college students, had kidnapped and murdered a 14-year-old boy in an attempt to commit the "perfect crime." Bryan quoted Darrow's defense of the pair, during which Darrow had blamed their crime on the fact that they had studied Nietzsche and what would come to be known as Social Darwinism in school. "I will guarantee you can go down to the University of Chicago today—into its big library and find over 1,000 volumes of Nietzsche, and I am sure I speak moderately. If this boy is to blame for this, where did he get it? Is there any blame attached because somebody took Nietzsche's philosophy seriously and fashioned his life on it? And there is no question in this case but what it is true. Then who is to blame? The university would be more to blame than he is. The scholars of the world would be more to blame than he is. The publishers of the world—and Nietzsche's books are published by one of the biggest publishers in the world— are more to blame than he is. Your honor, it is hardly fair to hang a 19-year old boy for the philosophy that was taught him at the university."

In response to Bryan, Darrow clarified that he had later added "I do not believe that the universities are to blame. I do not think they should be held responsible." However, the damage was done, especially when Bryan pointed out that Nietzsche was an enthusiastic student of Darwin.

When Bryan finished, it was not Darrow who rose to oppose him but Malone, who gave a rousing speech in favor of allowing the scientific evidence to be heard. He concluded, "There is never a duel with the truth. The truth always wins and we are not afraid of it. The truth is no coward. The truth does not need the law. The truth does not need the forces of government. The truth does not need Mr. Bryan. The truth is imperishable, eternal, and immortal, and needs no human agency to support it. We are ready to tell the truth as we understand it and we do not fear all the truth that they can present as facts. We are ready. We are ready. We feel we stand with progress. We feel we stand with science. We feel we stand with intelligence. We feel we stand with fundamental freedom in America. We are not afraid. Where is the fear? We meet it. Where is the fear? We defy it…"

According to Scopes, "The courtroom went wild when Malone finished. The heavy applause he had received during the speech was nothing compared to the crowd's reaction now at the end. The judge futilely called for order. … Malone took the crowd away from Bryan the Invincible, even though Bryan had wrapped up the audience and marked it his. Soon the spectators were cheering Malone. It was so dramatic that a transcript couldn't tell it."

Later, when they were alone, Bryan told Malone, "Dudley, that was the greatest speech I have ever heard." To that, Malone replied, "Thank you . . . I am sorry it was I who had to make it." Scopes later noted, "Bryan was never the same afterward and if there were any turning points in the trial that day was one. Dudley Field Malone had shattered his former chief's unbounded optimism, which Darrow is commonly credited with having done later in the trial. Bryan had reached his peak before Darrow ever got him on the stand. If anything, Malone's debilitating coup probably made Bryan want to go on the stand, in the vain hope of regaining some of his tarnished glory. … His reply to Bryan was the most dramatic event I have attended in my life. The intervening decades have produced nothing to equal it; nor do I expect to see anything like it in my remaining years."

Malone

After Malone, it was Stewart's turn to try to win the audience back to the prosecution. In making his less than exciting argument, he told the court, "They say it is a battle between religion and science, and in the name of God, I stand with religion because I want to know beyond this world that there may be an eternal happiness for me and for all." Stewart also spoke out against "teaching that infidelity, that agnosticism, that which breeds in the soul of the child, infidelity, atheism, and drives him from the Bible that his father and mother raised him by…I say, bar the door, and not allow science to enter."

Stewart saved his most scathing remarks for his chief opponent: "Mr. Darrow says he is an agnostic. He is the greatest criminal lawyer in American today. His courtesy is noticeable—his ability is known—and it is a shame, in my mind, in the sight of a great God, that mentality like his has strayed so far from the natural goal that it should follow—great God, the good that a man of his ability could have done if he had aligned himself with the forces of right instead of aligning himself with that which strikes its fangs at the very bosom of Christianity."

Chapter 6: Taking Every Advantage

"The prosecution is fighting desperately and taking every advantage of its superior knowledge of the quirks of local procedure. The defense is heating up and there are few exchanges of courtroom amenities. There will be a lot of oratory before it is all over and some loud and raucous bawling otherwise, and maybe more than one challenge to step outside. The cards seem to be stacked against poor Scopes, but there may be a joker in the pack. Four of the jurymen, as everyone knows, are Methodists, and a Methodist down here belongs to the extreme wing of liberals. Beyond him lie only the justly and incurably damned. What if one of those Methodists, sweating under the dreadful pressure of fundamentalist influence, jumps into the air, cracks his heels together and gives a defiant yell? What if the jury is hung? It will be a good joke on the fundamentalists if it happens, and an even better joke on the defense." - H. L. Mencken

In spite of Malone's best efforts, the following morning, the sixth day of the trial, Raulston ruled, "In the final analysis this court, after a most earnest and careful consideration, has reached the conclusions that under the provisions of the act involved in this case, it is made unlawful thereby to teach in the public schools of the state of Tennessee the theory that man descended from a lower order of animals. If the court is correct in this, then the evidence of experts would shed no light on the issues. Therefore, the court is content to sustain the motion of the attorney-general to exclude the expert testimony."

In addition to that ruling, however, the judge did agree to hear the expert witnesses with the jury sequestered away from the court. This led Bryan to demand the right to cross-examine the witnesses. Darrow objected to this, and the following exchange took place:

"Darrow—No, it is an effort to show prejudice. Nothing else. Has there been any effort to ascertain the truth in this case? Why not bring the jury and let us prove it?

"Court—Courts are a mockery—

"Darrow—They are often that, your honor.

"Court—When they permit cross-examination for the purpose of creating prejudice.

"Darrow—I submit, your honor there is no sort of question that they are not entitled to cross-examine, but all this evidence is to show what we expect to prove and nothing else, and can be nothing else.

"Court—I will say this: If the defense wants to put their proof in the record, in the form of affidavits, of course they can do that. If they put the witness on the stand and the state desires to cross-examine them, I shall expect them to do so.

"Darrow—We except to it and take an exception.

"Court—Yes, sir; always expect this court to rule correctly.

"Darrow—No, sir, we do not.

"Court—I suppose you anticipated it?

"Darrow—Otherwise we should not be taking our exceptions here, your honor. We expect to protect our rights in some other court. Now, that is plain enough, isn't it? Then we will make statements of what we expect to prove. Can we have the rest of the day to draft them?

"Court—I would not say—

"Darrow—If your honor takes a half day to write an opinion—

Court—I have not taken—

"Darrow—We want to make statements here of what we expect to prove. I do not understand why every request of the state and every suggestion of the prosecution should meet with an endless waste of time, and a bare suggestion of anything on our part should be immediately over-ruled.

"Court—I hope you do not mean to reflect upon Court?

"Darrow—Well, your honor has the right to hope.

"Court—I have the right to do something else, perhaps.

"Darrow—All right; all right."

Ultimately, Raulston granted Darrow the recess and thus the weekend to prepare his next gambit. Most people thought the case was over, and many left town, unaware that the best was yet to come.

Chapter 7: The Old Gladiator

"Bryan sat silent throughout the whole scene, his gaze fixed immovably on the witness. Now and then his face darkened and his eyes flashed, but he never uttered a sound. It was, to him, a string of blasphemies out of the devil's mass -- a dreadful series of assaults upon the only true religion. The old gladiator faced his real enemy at last. Here was a sworn agent and attorney of the science he hates and fears…. But let no one, laughing at him, underestimate the magic that lies in his black, malignant eye, his frayed but still eloquent voice. He can shake and inflame these poor ignoramuses as no other man among us can shake and inflame them, and he is desperately eager to order the charge. In Tennessee he is drilling his army. The big battles, he believes, will be fought elsewhere." - H. L. Mencken

When Monday morning, July 20, rolled around, the courtroom was so hot that Raulston ordered the court to convene under the shade trees on the courthouse lawn. The judge again demonstrated his flair for the dramatic by sending the jury out of earshot and then saying, "On last Friday, July 17, contempt and insult were expressed in this court, for the court and its orders and decrees…The court has withheld any action until passion had time to subdue…It has been my policy on the bench to be cautious and to endeavor to avoid hastily and rashly rushing to conclusions. But in the face of what I consider an unjustified expression of contempt for this court and its decrees, made by Clarence Darrow, on July 17, 1925, I feel that further forbearance would cease to be a virtue, and in an effort to protect the good name of my state, and to protect the dignity of the court…I am constrained and impelled to call upon the said Darrow, to know what he has to say why he should not be dealt with for contempt. Therefore, I hereby order that citation from this court be served upon the said Clarence Darrow, requiring him to appear in this court, at 9 o'clock a. m., Tuesday, July 21, 1925, and make answer to this citation. I also direct that upon the serving of the said citation that he be required to make and execute a good and lawful bond for $5,000 for his appearance from day to day upon said citation and not depart the court without leave."

Always playing an angle, Darrow replied, "Now, I do not know whether I could get anybody, your honor," only to have someone speak up on his behalf and assure the court, "There will be no trouble." The entry concluded, "Frank Spurlock, of Chattanooga, thereupon volunteered his services in the matter."

Wisely, Darrow soon thought better of the matter and, following the noon lunch break, requested to address the court and make a lengthy apology: "Your honor, quite apart from any question of what is right or wrong in this matter which your honor mentioned…and on my own account if nothing else was involved, I would feel that I ought to say what I am going to say. Of course, your honor will remember that whatever took place was hurried, one thing, followed another and the truth is I did not know just how it looked until I read over the minutes as your honor did and when I read them over I was sorry that I had said it. … I have been practicing law for forty-seven years and I have been pretty busy and most of the time in court I have had many a case where I have had to do what I have been doing here-fighting the public opinion of the people, in the community where I was trying the case- even in my own town and I never yet have in all my time had any criticism by the court for anything I have done in court. That is, I have tried to treat the court fairly and a little more than fairly because when I recognize the odds against me, I try to lean the other way the best I can and I don't think any such occasion ever arose before in my practice. I am not saying this, your honor, to influence you, but to put myself right. I do think, however, your honor, that I went further than I should have done. So far as its having been premeditated or made for the purpose of insult to the court I had not the slightest thought of that. I had not the slightest thought of that. One thing snapped out after another, as other lawyers have done in this case, not, however, where the judge was involved, and apologized for it afterwards…"

To his credit, Darrow extended his apology past the court and to the others he had insulted, adding that "so far as the people of Tennessee are concerned, your honor suggested that in your opinion-I don't know as I was ever in a community in my life where my religious ideas differed as widely from the great mass as I have found them since I have been in Tennessee. Yet I came here a perfect stranger and I can say what I have said before that I have not found upon anybody's part-any citizen here in this town or outside, the slightest discourtesy. I have been treated better, kindlier and more hospitably than I fancied would have been the case in the north, and that is due largely to the ideas that southern people have and they are, perhaps, more hospitable than we are up north... I am quite certain that the remark should not have been made and the court could not help taking notice of it and I am sorry that I made it ever since I got time to read it and I want to apologize to the court for it."

Darrow's apology hit its mark and was received with applause. Raulston then graciously accepted Darrow's apology: "My friends, and Col. Darrow, the Man that I believe came into the world to save man from sin, the Man that died on the cross that man might be redeemed, taught that it was godly to forgive and were it not for the forgiving nature of Himself I would fear for man. The Savior died on the cross pleading with God for the men who crucified Him. I believe in that Christ. I believe in these principles. I accept Col. Darrow's apology. I am sure his remarks were not premeditated. I am sure that if he had time to have thought and deliberated he would not have spoken those words. He spoke those words, perhaps, just at a moment when he felt that he had suffered perhaps one of the greatest disappointments of his life when the court had held against him. Taking that view of it, I feel that I am justified in speaking for the people of the great state that I represent when I speak as I do to say to him that we forgive him and we forgot it and we commend him to go back home and learn in his heart the words of the Man who said: 'If you thirst come unto Me and I will give thee life.'" Having concluded this portion of the day, Raulston gave everyone a much needed break from the heat by ordering the trial once more moved outside.

Once they were outdoors, Hays began to present the evidence of his expert witnesses, beginning with a statement from Rabbi Dr. Herman Rosenwasser, a well-known Hebrew scholar. Next, he spoke of the work of Dr. Herman Murkett, the pastor of the First Methodist Church in nearby Chattanooga. These were followed by many other similar statements, all meant to show that there was no real conflict between the Christian faith and evolution. Since the jury would not hear these arguments, they were obviously not aimed at the case but at the national debate they would spark.

It must have seemed to many in the audience that the trial was proving to be a great disappointment. After presenting extensive expert testimony, however, Hays stood up and announced, "The defense desires to call Mr. Bryan as a witness, and, of course, the only question here is whether Mr. Scopes taught what these children said he taught, we recognize what Mr. Bryan says as a witness would not be very valuable. We think there are other questions involved, and we should want to take Mr. Bryan's testimony for the purposes of our record, even if your honor thinks it is not admissible in general, so we wish to call him now."

After some back and forth between those around him, Bryan announced, "If your honor please, I insist that Mr. Darrow can be put on the stand, and Mr. Malone and Mr. Hays." Bryan then asked, "Where do you want me to sit?" Word quickly spread that Bryan himself was going to testify, and the crowd around the courthouse grew to more than 2,000.

A picture of Darrow (standing) cross-examining Bryan (seated)

At first, the exchange was pretty tame:

"DARROW-You have given considerable study to the Bible, haven't you, Mr. Bryan?

BRYAN-Yes, sir, I have tried to.

DARROW-Well, we all know you have, we are not going to dispute that at all. But you have written and published articles almost weekly, and sometimes have made interpretations of various things?

BRYAN-I would not say interpretations, Mr. Darrow, but comments on the lesson.

DARROW-If you comment to any extent these comments have been interpretations.

BRYAN-I presume that my discussion might be· to some extent interpretations, but they have not been primarily intended as interpretations."

Suddenly, Darrow's tactics changed. According to Reed, "The courtyard was packed. There were not enough seats to hold all of the people and they were standing around. The benches had been set up all in front of the stand so we had a seat right in front of Darrow and Bryan. And I was all set to hear the great trial going on. ... William Jennings Bryan was sitting there with a big palm fan and a handkerchief in his hand. Darrow is in his shirtsleeves with red suspenders, which he wore. He jumped up right in front of him, took hold of his red suspenders and flipped them, and said, 'Do you really believe that that whale swallowed Jonah?'" Bryan was ready for such a question and replied, "I believe it, and I believe in a God who can make a whale and can make a man and make both do what He pleases."

After a brief argument, Darrow moved on to other questions, such as "Did Joshua lengthen the day by making the sun or the earth stand still?" In explaining his attitude about such matters, Bryan was eloquent in response: "I can take a glass of water that would fall to the ground without the strength of my hand and to the extent of the glass of water I can overcome the law of gravitation and lift it up. Whereas without my hand it would fall to the ground. If my puny hand can overcome the law of gravitation, the most universally understood, to that extent, I would set power to the hand of Almighty God that made the universe."

Darrow moved on to other questions, including extensive ones related to the age of the Earth, but throughout the questioning, Bryan kept his head, at one point indirectly reminding Darrow that he was not the only great mind in the room. "I had occasion to study Confucianism when I went to China. I got all I could find about what Confucius said, and then I bought a book that told us what Menches said about what Confucius said, and I found that there were several direct and strong contrasts between the teachings of Jesus and the teaching of Confucius. In the first place, one of his followers asked if there was any word that would express all that was necessary to know in the relations of life, and he said, 'Isn't reciprocity such a word?' I know of no better illustration of the difference between Christianity and Confucianism than the contrast that is brought out there. Reciprocity is a calculating selfishness. If a person does something for you, you do something for him and keep it even. That is the basis of the philosophy of Confucius. Christ's doctrine was not reciprocity. We were told to help people not in proportion as they had helped us--not in proportion as they might have helped us, but in proportion to their needs, and there is all the difference in the world between a religion that teaches you just to keep even with other people and the religion that teaches you to spend yourself for other people and to help them as they need help."

Of course, Darrow was not interested in the morality of Christian teachings but in the "science" of the Bible. Thus, he continued with questions such as "Did God make Eve out of Adam's rib?" At first, Bryan did a pretty good job of using humor to deflect the questioning:

>"Mr. Bryan, do you believe that the first woman was Eve?"

>"Yes, I do."

>"Do you believe she was literally made out of Adam's rib?

>"I do, Mr. Darrow."

>"Did you ever discover where Cain got his wife?"

>"No, sir. I leave you agnostics to hunt for her."

The problem was that humor, while it made him popular with his local audience, did nothing to impress the people across the country who were listening to the exchange over the radio, and it was the masses who Darrow was after. As historian Paul Boyer noted, "It is fascinating to read the transcript of the trial. Bryan had the local audience very much in the palm of his hand. Time and again in the transcript when Bryan responds to one of Darrow's questions, the person who was recording the events would write 'applause...laughter'' over and over again. Bryan was their champion and they were egging him on. It was very much like a sporting event. You know, cheering your hero. And I think Bryan won the local battle overwhelmingly. Darrow of course understood that the real battle was being fought out nationwide, and he was playing to a larger audience."

A similar line of questions continued:

>"Mr. Bryan, do you think the earth was created in six days?"

>"No, Sir. Not six days of twenty-four hours."

>"The creation might have been going on for a very long time?"

>"Yes, Mr. Darrow. It might have continued for millions of years."

Finally, an exasperated Bryan stumbled and cried out, "It doesn't make any difference to us whether God created the world in six days, six years, six million years, or even six hundred million years." This was the moment that Darrow had been waiting for, and he swooped in: "Well if you can interpret those things in the Bible, why can't we interpret the story of the creation of humans in an evolutionary sense?" Young Eloise Reed remembered, "He just kept pushing him and pushing him. You know I wanted to get up off of that bench and go up there and kick him. It was just, I imagine people out there in the audience felt the same way to make him hush. The thing was, he was attacking the Bible. Finally the judge said to him, 'Well, what do you mean. You are harassing your own witness. What you are asking him has nothing to do with the issue of this trial. We want you to put a stop to it.'"

At this point, Bryan himself spoke up: "Your honor, I think I can shorten this testimony. The only purpose Mr. Darrow has is to slur at the Bible, but I will answer his question. I will answer it all at once, and I have no objection in the world, I want the world to know that this man, who does not believe in a God, is trying to use a court in Tennessee to slur at it, and while it will require time, I am willing to take it." To this, Darrow replied, "I object to your statement. I am exempting you on your fool ideas that no intelligent Christian on earth believes." With that comment ringing in the ears of the nation, Raulston banged his gavel and announced, "Court is adjourned until 9 o'clock tomorrow morning."

Chapter 8: With Great Skill

"[Darrow's] conduct of the case, in fact, was adept and intelligent from beginning to end. It is hard, in retrospect, to imagine him improving it. He faced immense technical difficulties. In order to get out of the clutches of the village Dogberry and before judges of greater intelligence he had to work deliberately for the conviction of his client. In order to evade the puerile question of that client's guilt or innocence and so bring the underlying issues before the country, he had to set up a sham battle on the side lines. ... It seems to me that he accomplished all of these things with great skill. Scopes was duly convicted, and the constitutional questions involved in the law will now be heard by competent judges and decided without resort to prayer and moving pictures. The whole world has been made familiar with the issues, and the nature of the menace that Fundamentalism offers to civilization is now familiar to every schoolboy. And Bryan was duly scotched.... All this was accomplished, in infernal weather, by a man of sixty-eight, with the scars of battles all over him." - H. L. Mencken

Tuesday morning, July 21, dawned hot and humid, just as the previous days had. The jurors wondered if they would actually be allowed to hear any testimony, while Raulston wondered what would happen next. Bryan was excited, looking forward to another day in which he could testify to his faith, but Darrow arose knowing that he was about to play his last card.

After Raulston called the court to order, he announced, "As I see it after due deliberation, I feel that Mr. Bryan's testimony cannot aid the higher court in determining that question. If the question before the higher court involved the issue as to what evolution was or as to how God created man, or created the earth or created the universe, this testimony might be relevant, but those questions are not before the court and so taking this view of it, I am pleased to expunge this testimony given by Mr. Bryan on yesterday from the records of this court and it will not be further considered."

With his previous testimony struck from the record, Bryan now had only his closing arguments to leave to posterity, but he would also lose those. Darrow addressed the court, "We have already been here quite a while and I say it in perfectly good faith we have no witnesses to offer, no proof to offer on the issues that the court has laid down here that Mr. Scopes did teach what the children said he taught, that man descended from a lower order of animals- we do not mean to contradict that and I think to save time we will ask the court to bring in the jury and instruct the jury to find the defendant guilty. We make no objection to that and it will save a lot of time and I think that should be done."

Needless to say, this was a blow to Bryan, who may or may not have realized this was his last campaign. Disappointed, he told the court, "I shall have to trust to the justness of the press, which reported what was said yesterday, to report what I will say, not to the court, but to the press in answer to the charge scattered broadcast over the world and I shall also avail myself of the opportunity to give to the press, not to the court, the questions that I would have asked had I been permitted to call the attorneys on the other side."

Given the exclusion of so much testimony, it only took the jury nine minutes to reach the foregone conclusion that Scopes was indeed guilty of teaching evolution, and that he would be fined under the law. When given a chance to respond, Scopes spoke for the first time in court, saying, "Your honor, I feel that I have been convicted of violating an unjust statute. I will continue in the future, as I have in the past, to oppose this law in any way I can. Any other action would be in violation of my ideal of academic freedom, that is, to teach the truth as guaranteed in our constitution, of personal and religious freedom. I think the fine is unjust."

Of course, as had been the case throughout the trial, people really wanted to hear the final comments of the two main combatants. Bryan spoke first, and briefly, saying, among other things, "Here has been fought out a little case of little consequence as a case, but the world is interested because it raises an issue, and that issue will someday be settled right, whether it is settled on our side or the other side. It is going to be settled right. There can be no settlement of a great cause without discussion, and people will not discuss a cause until their attention is drawn to it, and the value of this trial is not in any incident of the trial, it is not because of anybody who is attached to it, either in an official way or as counsel on either side. Human beings are mighty small, your honor. We are apt to magnify the personal element and we sometimes become inflated with our importance, but the world little cares for man as an individual. He is born, he works, he dies, but causes go on forever, and we who participated in this case may congratulate ourselves that we have attached ourselves to a mighty issue."

Darrow also spoke: "Of course, there is much that Mr. Bryan has said that is true. And nature-nature, I refer to does not choose any special setting for more events. I fancy that the place where the Magna Carta was wrested from the barons in England was a very small place, probably not as big as Dayton. But events come along as they come along. I think this case will be remembered because it is the first case of this sort since we stopped trying people in America for witchcraft because here we have done our best to turn back the tide that has sought to force itself upon this--upon this modern world, of testing every fact in science by a religious dictum. That is all I care to say."

Finally, reserving the last word for himself, Judge Raulston concluded, "My fellow citizens, I recently read somewhere what I think was a definition of a great man, and that was this: That he possesses a passion to know the truth and have the courage to declare it in the face of all opposition. It is easy enough, my friends, to have a passion to find a truth, or to find a fact, rather, that coincides with our preconceived notions and ideas, but it sometimes takes courage to search diligently for a truth, that may destroy our preconceived notions and ideas.... I am glad to have had these gentlemen with us. This little talk of mine comes from my heart, gentlemen. I have had some difficult problems to decide in this lawsuit, and I only pray to God that I have decided them right. If I have not, the higher courts will find the mistake. But if I failed to decide them right, it was for the want of legal learning, and legal attainment, and not for the want of a disposition to do everybody justice. We are glad to have you with us."

Clarence Darrow would go on to enjoy many more years of practice, but he would never face Bryan again; the following Sunday, after attending church in Dayton, the famous orator went back to his room, lay down for an afternoon nap, and never woke up. When someone tried to blame Darrow for breaking Bryan's heart and killing him, Darrow sharply retorted, "Broken heart, hell, he died of a busted belly!"

Though it has long been forgotten, Scopes' defense appealed the ruling to Tennessee's Supreme Court, where it made many similar arguments. The court rejected the defense's arguments that the law was too vague and unconstitutional, holding, "Evolution, like prohibition, is a broad term. In recent bickering, however, evolution has been understood to mean the theory which holds that man has developed from some pre-existing lower type. This is the popular significance of evolution, just as the popular significance of prohibition is prohibition of the traffic in intoxicating liquors. It was in that sense that evolution was used in this act. It is in this sense that the word will be used in this opinion, unless the context otherwise indicates. It is only to the theory of the evolution of man from a lower type that the act before us was intended to apply, and much of the discussion we have heard is beside this case."

The court also held that the Butler Act did not violate the freedom of expression or the establishment of a state religion: "We are not able to see how the prohibition of teaching the theory that man has descended from a lower order of animals gives preference to any religious establishment or mode of worship. So far as we know, there is no religious establishment or organized body that has in its creed or confession of faith any article denying or affirming such a theory. So far as we know, the denial or affirmation of such a theory does not enter into any recognized mode of worship. Since this cause has been pending in this court, we have been favored, in addition to briefs of counsel and various amici curiae, with a multitude of resolutions, addresses, and communications from scientific bodies, religious factions, and individuals giving us the benefit of their views upon the theory of evolution. Examination of these contributions indicates that Protestants, Catholics, and Jews are divided among themselves in their beliefs, and that there is no unanimity among the members of any religious establishment as to this subject. Belief or unbelief in the theory of evolution is no more a characteristic of any religious establishment or mode of worship than is belief or unbelief in the wisdom of the prohibition laws. It would appear that members of the same churches quite generally disagree as to these things."

However, the court did overturn the fine against Scopes, and Chief Justice Grafton Green expressed the hope that the infamous trial would go away: "The court is informed that the plaintiff in error is no longer in the service of the state. We see nothing to be gained by prolonging the life of this bizarre case. On the contrary, we think that the peace and dignity of the state, which all criminal prosecutions are brought to redress, will be the better conserved by the entry of a nolle prosequi herein. Such a course is suggested to the Attorney General."

Over 40 years later, the U.S. Supreme Court ruled in *Epperson v. Arkansas* (1968) that the kind of prohibitions put forth by legislation like the Butler Act were in fact unconstitutional because they violated the First Amendment's establishment clause barring the establishment of a state religion. By then, the Butler Act had already been repealed in Tennessee, Bryan and Darrow had been dead for decades. and John Scopes would be dead within two years.

Online Resources

Other books about 20th century American history by Charles River Editors

Other books about the Scopes Trial on Amazon

Bibliography

de Camp, L. Sprague (1968), *The Great Monkey Trial*, Doubleday.

Conkin, Paul K. (1998), *When All the Gods Trembled: Darwinism, Scopes, and American Intellectuals*.

Larson, Edward J. (1997), *Summer for the Gods: The Scopes Trial and America's Continuing Debate Over Science and Religion*, BasicBooks.

Moran, Jeffrey P. (2002), *The Scopes Trial: A Brief History with Documents*, Bedford/St. Martin's.

Scopes, John T.; Presley, James (1967), *Center of the Storm: Memoirs of John T. Scopes*, Henry Holt & Company.

The World's Most Famous Court Trial, State of Tennessee vs. John Thomas Scopes: Complete Stenographic Report of the Court.

Tompkins, Jerry R. (1968), *D-Days at Dayton: Reflections on the Scopes Trial*, Louisiana State University Press.

Made in the USA
Middletown, DE
06 December 2019